Pink
Waves

ALSO BY SAWAKO NAKAYASU

POETRY
Some Girls Walk Into The Country They Are From
The Ants
*Mouth: Eats Color—Sagawa Chika Translations, Anti-Translations, and
    Originals*
Texture Notes
Hurry Home Honey
Nothing fictional but the accuracy or arrangement
So we have been given time Or

PROSE
Say Translation Is Art

TRANSLATION
Yi Sang: Collected Works by Yi Sang, with Jack Jung, Don Mee Choi,
    Joyelle McSweeney
The Collected Poems of Chika Sagawa by Chika Sagawa
Costume en Face by Tatsumi Hijikata
Time of Sky and *Castles in the Air* by Ayane Kawata
For the Fighting Spirit of the Walnut by Takashi Hiraide

What carries stillness? Who will hold "your wild"? What is: "elegy function"? Sawako Nakayasu's *Pink Waves* is an experience of questions becoming artifacts. The speaker asks: "how will i locate expansiveness in touch"? By "dreamlight," a reader is trained, by this speaker, in a process of listening that's both a "pledge of silence" and the recognition that "we come to a limit and stop where it fits." Is this "genre trouble"? Nakayasu has written a book a writer could read, orienting to the desk, to the "passing moment," in turn. This is grounding. This is beautiful.

—BHANU KAPIL

In a deliberate lyricism of regathering, tethering, and receding precedence, in a perpetual canon that keeps spilling and sifting and replenishing what feels like dancing, in a series of breaks weaving wave and snap into writing that listens, Sawako Nakayasu takes the measure of the enjoyment we derive from sensing and making sense of this wasteland of bandwidth and access. *Pink Waves* is a delicate instrument. Its spare beauty picks up everything.

— FRED MOTEN

author of *The Universal Machine (consent not to be a single being)*

Pink Waves deepens my immense admiration for Sawako Nakayasu's poems and translations. Expansive, working across genres, she always pushes her writing into new places. In *Pink Waves*, she has found another way to rigorously clear a space for herself or, perhaps more accurately, her many selves, attaining a fresh perspective. Registering the world crashing into her life, we hear and learn the different languages, from Wôpanâak to Chinese, that flow around her, as well as encounter references to— and echoes of—Adam Pendleton's collage text Black Dada, Valerie Solanas' radical feminist SCUM Manifesto, Sol LeWitt's "Paragraphs on Conceptual Art," and Ron Silliman's groundbreaking *Ketjak*. She uses collage to give a resilient, changing shape to our relentless influx of chaos, and the resulting feelings of anxiety, passion, anger, and love stirred up in us. Turning detritus into sensuous music, Nakayasu's greatness arises from [undertaking] "Experiments in Joy," à la Gabrielle Civil, to find a way to live in the here and now.

— JOHN YAU
author of *Genghis Chan on Drums*

Pink
Waves

Sawako Nakayasu

OMNIDAWN PUBLISHING
OAKLAND, CALIFORNIA
2022

Cover art by Naomi Kawanishi Reis

Text set in Adobe Jenson Pro

Cover and interior design by Sawako Nakayasu and Laura Joakimson

Library of Congress Cataloging-in-Publication Data

Names: Nakayasu, Sawako, 1975- author.
Title: Pink waves / Sawako Nakayasu.
Description: Oakland, California : Omnidawn Publishing, 2022. | Summary:
  "Pink Waves is a poem of radiant elegy and quiet protest, in loose
  sonata form. It accrues lines written in conversation with Waveform by
  Amber DiPietra and Denise Leto, and microtranslations of syntax in
  "Black Dada" by Adam Pendleton, itself written via Ron Silliman's
  Ketjak. Moving through the shifting surfaces of inarticulable loss, and
  the granular edges of dark, sad matter, Nakayasu completed the book in
  the presence of audience members in a three-day durational performance.
  Held within: a shimmering haunting of tenderness, hunger, and detritus.
  "We ate them.""-- Provided by publisher.

Identifiers: LCCN 2022035012 | ISBN 9781632430984 (trade paperback)
Subjects: LCGFT: Poetry.
Classification: LCC PS3614.A575 P56 2022 | DDC 811/.6--dc23/eng/20220722
LC record available at https://lccn.loc.gov/2022035012

Published by Omnidawn Publishing, Oakland, California
www.omnidawn.com   (510) 237-5472
10 9 8 7 6 5 4 3 2 1
ISBN: 978-1-63243-098-4

for the ones we lost

and the loves we love

A

1

it was a wave all along

2

it was a wave all along

a passing moment reveals itself to have cued the long apology

3

it was a wave all along

sliding between the heat of now and surrender

a passing moment reveals itself to have cued the long apology

i sat with a friend and the loss of her child

4

it was a wave all along

a passing moment reveals itself to have cued the long apology

i sat with a friend and the loss of her child

sliding between the heat of now and surrender

and then somebody holds your wild you

closer to the range

the specs of a body don't reveal what it means, so which body do you want to wear today?

the extent that we need another dollar

5

it was a wave all along

a passing moment reveals itself to have cued the long apology

the extent that we need another dollar

it's haptic; it's your membrane

sliding between the heat of now and surrender

and then somebody holds your wild you

which parts available for naming

atop a sharp manicured nail

a quiet neck is often mismeasured as discomfort which is
indifferent to the noise of the world

the desk is positioned at the wrong height

e-mails insert pointed arrows to indicate previous utterance
in a moment of refrain

the desk is a spacial deadline

replacing a hip

she was an elegy function; she happened at once; she pitched

so did i love

these goals are a great carrier of stillness

6

it was a wave all along

a passing moment reveals itself to have cued the long apology

now i am at odds with myself

sliding between the heat of now and surrender

she was an elegy function; she happened at once; she pitched

so did i love

e-mails insert pointed arrows to indicate previous utterance
in a moment of refrain

closer to the range

the desk is a spacial deadline

and then somebody holds your wild you

it's haptic; it's your membrane

cantilevered muscles

the extent that we need another dollar

atop a sharp manicured nail

which parts available for naming

i want the drifting organisms of the space between

i want the slightly eroded quicksand moat to protect us all
from impending waves

i want a decidedly animal resolution

a slip of concentration in the predicate vicinity is cause for a
public lapse, crashing one wave after another

the desk is positioned at the wrong height

she was an elegy function; she happened at once; she pitched

the assumption of her back

the formal struggle of a vertical field of grass

did your status change?

yes we are warm

i want a very animal claim

when the goals bring the stillness, a new sound erupts as if out of nowhere

i think that some people just never stop writing

sediments and molecules get inflamed more often than you think

hip replacing hip

internal findings move in super slow motion beneath the bedroom window

cede of control

7

it was a wave all along

a passing moment reveals itself to have cued the long apology

sliding between the heat of now and surrender

now i am at odds with myself

she was an elegy function; she happened at once; she pitched

the formal struggle of a vertical field of grass

and then somebody holds your wild you

i need the drifting organisms of the space between

i need the slightly eroded quicksand moat to protect us all
from impending waves

i need a decidedly animal resolution

cantilevered muscles

when the goals bring the stillness, a new sound erupts as if out of nowhere

some people just never stop writing

Black Dada, black dada

this is a snap and tether, i assure you

to walk there is to flank the path with impolite noises, lift back a head raring with deaf rage determined to largeness loudness a length of time enough time for all to reach for their Swiss umbrellas

i had a nice dick; the sky is blue

i wanted you to see it, want it

yes we are warm; i touch the quiet edges of your body into a spin

i need a very animal claim

it's haptic; it's your membrane

the extent that we need another dollar

which parts available for naming atop a sharp manicured nail

how are we to define this node

what makes you wave at my cocked head in the pool

what do you want to bang against

do you think that if i brought you more and more endless bluegreen ovals, then far below the surface you could jam an entire shark, following the manatee, into your body and you could translate that into this touch, that blow, and linger in the deep?

i want the detached musculature to resist

i need an explanation

what did you bring when they turned the grass to vertical?

hip replacing hip

developing scab

imperialist narrator turns the volume up against the position the principle the susurration

the goal of stillness is to link up the spectral and the membrane to a higher form of visibility

uninvited noise is to be held back with steep consequences

we want to make noise

she was an elegy function; she happened at once; she pitched her loud voice to the waves i want to enter the space between

i need a constant morning, a kick in my mouth and coffee

a fullness and mouth for two

body with terms

time capsule

Black Dada is a way to talk about the future while talking about the past; it is our present moment

a slip of concentration in the predicate vicinity is cause for a public lapse, crashing one wave after another

magical girls of the swell

did your status change?

the steady abiding, the deafgain

e-mails insert pointed arrows to indicate previous utterance in a moment of refrain

so did i love this

the desk is a spacial deadline

the goals are positioned at the wrong height

line, hold to it

closer to the range

i want a person to drown in or mirror laughter

green blade of a grassy field

self into self

better able to introduce a path towards comfort

how will i locate expansiveness in touch

refuge

snap

we ate them

8

it was a wave all along

she was an elegy function; she happened at once; she pitched

a passing moment reveals itself to have cued the long apology

the formal struggle of a vertical field of grass

now i am at odds with myself

Black Dada

Black Dada was written by Adam Pendleton

The *Black Dada Reader* is a collage by Adam Pendleton in the form of a book

Black Dada is not mine

But Black Dada made this book it crashes into my performance Tuesday May 14 2019 11:50 am

can you hold it

do you hear it

is it hard enough

do you like it

do you want more

is this the right angle

is it here

are you breathing

is it you

are you here

does it hold

is it too heavy

what about dinner

fish or cigarettes

or coffee

bed of fog

i do not claim Black Dada but i know that certain uses of the word love is a trap

internal findings move in super slow motion beneath the bedroom window

hideous art, that which is dead

reflux is the new register upon which we vote

music was used by the children like this: they shout song lyrics into the air and make friends with those who turn their heads

one can aspire to be almost as good as the children on bicycles

back in the dirt: naïvely rooting around

back in the dirt: successive generations

back in the dirt: all the loves i have loved

back in the dirt: bring a flower when you visit in case the rest is unintelligible

you you you night you you

that is how she said it

i need you to see it, want it

i need an animal resolution

i need the slightly eroded quicksand moat to protect us all
from impending waves

i need to enter the space between

i need the drifting organisms of the space between

in the late 1960s Valerie Solanas and Sol LeWitt sat down
in New York to write manifestos while others feared for
their lives because of their manifestations

in 1967 Solanas self-published SCUM Manifesto and
sold the mimeographed copies on the street; Sol LeWitt's
Paragraphs on Conceptual Art were published in *Artforum*

in 1969 Sirhan Sirhan shot Bobby Kennedy no that was
1968

alone over my dead fire

in part i pass by pursuing your betters

white Pablo, black Pablo

in 1970 the student Irina Dunn scrawled a woman needs a
man like a fish needs a bicycle on a bathroom door

in 1960 the poem became a functional object, except not for
most of us

women marched in 2017, in pink hats and not pink hats

as i write this i consider the upcoming first lockdown, which war against which rational this time this time

what is the 1960s hanging from the hot bosom of the 2010s

i still notice Gertrude Stein but would have steered clear of her ego

seemingly large beauty or glitter or the dark whip of power, Stacey Tran has left

in the wake of accumulated war neverending

mass breathing

dislocation

burnt confabulation

Black Pablo

conceptual artists do not hold hands they do not have hands not in that way

conceptual artists do not march they do not have feet and legs not in that way

conceptual artists do not make faces they do not have feelings not in that way

history is a cube in the foreground i prick my ears to the
back

you you you you you fire

a slip of concentration in the predicate vicinity is cause for a
public lapse, crashing one wave after another

line, hold to it

closer to the range

i want the detached musculature to resist

kick in my mouth

i want a person to drown in or mirror laughter

e-mails insert pointed arrows to indicate previous utterance
in a moment of refrain

so do i love

the desk is a spatial deadline

the desk is positioned at the wrong height, I will stretch and
fix it for you

the central rhythms of partial identities

the sound must never impose itself over the images, or
override or shout down

any alerts on the table must answer to the desk

emancipatory or reactionary figures are not allowed to
coexist

substandard caprice, horrid little boys, and schooners of any
kind are actively discouraged

a woman lies in the middle of the central aching pasture
from which she cannot get up

alienation of hybrid bodies and terms are forbidden but
deeply commonplace

an intervention is requested but unfulfilled

when i was willing to wait thirty minutes, two hours, ten
years for you

green blade of a grassy field

self into self

cantilevered muscles of joy

fact bandwidth

snap

refuge

a quiet neck is often mismeasured as discomfort which is indifferent to the noise of the world

the assumption of her back

how will I locate expansiveness in touch

the extent that we need another dollar

do you think that if i brought you more and more endless bluegreen ovals, then far below the surface you could jam an entire shark, following the manatee, into your body and you could translate that into this touch, that blow, and linger in the deep?

if time drops here my function is to bewilder it

i need an explanation

better able to introduce a path towards comfort

Black Dada is our present moment

not canceling means keeping some waves; the machine-made spine can still be heard in this iteration and the next

that is to say my bidding is never enough

the solitude of my resistant pitch motions towards commitments that merit utopian amorous interpretations

a politics is mortar and muzzle

the steady abiding, the deafgain

time capsule

we want to make noise

hip replacement hip

internal findings move in super slow motion beneath the
bedroom window

cede of control

imperialist narrator turns the volume up against the position
the principle the susurration

i need a constant morning, a kick in my mouth and coffee

a fullness and mouth for two

i propose an evasion of inordinately large demands

no i do not speak English

the ringing sound you hear is the ordinary wait time
until the swelling in your ear returns to its dreary normal
pressures in keeping with the patterns of the infectious edges
of the body

here is a higher discernment

since when is discernment the right thing to desire

no and no

what is it that attracts you to so many creatures

sitting on the banks of a new book, i abolish the
conventionally attractive

did you know i have a nice dick, and the sky is blue

what i fail to embody can be passed along, recycled

do you know what i fail like

variegate me if you can, you don't have to eat it, art is there
it is, i adore you, i was wrong, if i say something i will still be
wrong so i learn to hang with it, i miss you, i fall and brush
the dirty sidewalk off my sleeve

now i am at odds with myself

solitude of my pitch

we ate them

B

1

snap

2

was that you

or the genre trouble

3

no and no

dorsal recumbent

transitlight

egression, delay

4

dissipate this

occasional light

stranger into self

nothing in reserve

does it connect

can you warfare connect it

is it ceremony enough

delivered light language world

5

is it too infectious

breathing en masse

facts of a bandwidth

material authorial clutter

flesh and stargazing hoax

Adam Golaski is going away

is this the right thought experiment

are you breathing or are you myopic

substrata, substrata

no end to the territory

closer to capitulation

stigmata, big stigmata

proximity to falsification

a hipper replacement

geometry of affect

it was hardly a pleasure

6

Qianxun Chen is going away

collimation dreamlight

that is how she said it rolled

black Pablo, white Pablo

going away is not even death

let me answer to the table

the unrepentant table

no i do not speak English

yes my nice dick is mine

normalized thickness of light

the backyard of my psychosis

i need an animal resolution

pink hats don't die so easy

light intermission continues

green blade of a grassy field

cantilevered muscles of joy

a dorsal assumption

let me commiserate a pledge of silence

here is a higher discernment

i am now at odds with myself

you set the conceptual line on fire

who are you, persona non grata

a politics is mortar and muzzle

the sun is saluted again and again

erotic anemone in darkest tunnel-light

an intervention died before it landed

your history of art my history of art

Black Dada is our present moment

make space for a disparate everything

human institutions, those which are dead

back in the dirt: successive generations

we come to a limit and stop where it fits

7

in cold i pass, fashion a wave

i want the detached musculature to resist

betweenness as an overarching capacity

that is to say my bidding is never enough

this is a catastrophe this is a broad claim

invisible light, i hold it and slip it to you

Black Dada as written by Adam Pendleton

those frogs fit right into their narrative ploy

i need to articulate my suspicion of foul play

in the wake of accumulated war neverending

i want a person to drown in or mirror my laughter

no imposition of sounds impossible to forget

intervention is requested but unfulfilled

dancing in a body that is inherently threatening

better able to launch a path towards comfort

i don't need any more inhabitants to my body

risk of being misread maligned and left behind

i need the drifting organisms of the long machine

i steal crumbs from your mouth to bake my own bread

tending disappearance a garden within a garden

i do not need to own it, the shimmer of completion

what is it that attracts you to so many creatures

someone walks in carrying a clear jar of silence

is there an incorrect occasion to take your highest temperature

alarm bells go off when the dancer touches truth

did you know i have a nice kick, and the sky is blue

i still have no idea what has happened in between

those who are most shy discover themselves in performance

noble futurelight celebrating the reinvention of everybody

ich sterbe versus you just lost me, when people go away

what is the 1960s hanging from the hot bosom of the 2010s

Erica Hunt's poetry is rehearsal for alternative worlds

i don't need your currents your headlines your dispatch

i need a constant morning, a kick in my mouth and coffee

my texture begs your question don't roll your eyes at me

history is a cube in the foreground i prick my ears to the back

they all watch him as he stretches his neck and lifts up his head

i still notice Gertrude Stein but would have steered clear of her ego

when i was willing to wait thirty minutes, two hours, ten years for

an irreparable release of all the frogs in all the classrooms in the

one can aspire to be almost as good as the children on interstellar

conceptual artists do not hold hands they do not have hands not in

internal findings move in super slow motion beneath the bedroom

the book starting with Adam Pendleton's Black Dada will come to

seemingly large beauty or glitter or the dark whip of power

the unjust occasion for this book is not typical but it scorches just you

country

bicycles

that way

window

an end

the same

conceptual artists do not make faces they do not have feelings not

the particularities of this injustice call for a revenge full of love, i

alienation of hybrid bodies and terms are forbidden but deeply

a frog is being dissected and my heart is red my people are fish the

she is seemingly nothing but a pigeonhole, but furtively she is on

in the shade of a plant that refuses to die, a small boy rescues a

your radar signature the trace of your body's path in space the

substandard caprice, horrid little boys, and schooners of any kind

i remind myself not to make assumptions about the owner of the

as i write this i consider the upcoming first lockdown, which war

in 1970 Irina Dunn scrawled a woman needs a man like a fish needs

But Black Dada made this book it crashes into my performance

not canceling means keeping some waves; the machine-made spine

music was used by the children like this: they shout song lyrics into

in the late 1960s Valerie Solanas and Sol LeWitt sat down in New
of their manifestations

in that way

can fill it yes you can

commonplace

invitation is here

the highest slopes

creature from the trash

evidence of alternative light

are actively discouraged

silence versus the owner of the jar

against which rational this time this time

a bicycle on a bathroom door

Tuesday May 14 2019 11:50 am

can still be heard in this iteration and the next

the air and make friends with those who turn their heads

York to write manifestos while others feared for their lives because

language poets put their politics in aesthetics and wrested power
power to the intersection

this may not appear that joyful but it is joyful to have a word in
alone and together

that ringing sound you hear is the ordinary wait time until the
patterns of the infectious edges of the body

from the establishment, but it's up to their offspring to take that

this life to redefine the performance of a poem to change my claims,

swelling in your ear resumes its banal pressures, keeping with the

do you think that if i brought you more and more endless blue-
following the manatee, into your body and you could translate that

variegate me, you don't have to eat it, art is there it is, i adore you,
with it, i miss you, i fall and brush the dirty sidewalk off my sleeve

in 2019 private equity investor Victor Lance Vescovo traveled 11
spoon worm, a pink snailfish, as well as the sharp edges of a man-

in 1967 Solanas self-published her SCUM Manifesto and sold
Conceptual Art were published in *Artforum*

the shoelaces of audience members who identify as such are covertly
see the light

i respect the need for bicycles and bathrooms but suspect the voice of

yesterday i wrote a letter to which i received a response in the form

a slip of concentration in the predicate vicinity is cause for a public

the solitude of my resistant pitch gestures towards commitments

Netop means friend in Wôpanâak, péngyou means friend in

frogs die easily in sites of abundance; a road in Kusano Shimpei's

i need to enter the blue space between whatever measures of time green ovals, then far below the surface you could jam an entire shark, into this touch, that blow, and linger in a truer deep?

i was wrong, if i say something i will still be wrong so i learn to hang

km into the depths of the Mariana Trench and saw some shrimp, a made object

mimeographed copies on the street; Sol LeWitt's Paragraphs on

tied together and when they try to run out of fear, that is when they

an external traducer, contest the outcome the wrongness still murks

of a call and response, called to conduct *Experiments in Joy*

lapse, crashing one wave after another

that merit utopian amorous manifestations

Chinese, mindful how you wield that word

Iwaki is covered in frogkill

the body requires to reassemble itself

a quiet neck is often mismeasured as discomfort which is

anyone who enters can witness my quiet protest i release it into the

empirical narrator turns the volume up against the ambition the

a woman lies in the middle of the central aching pasture from

avant-garde poet Takagai Hiroya wailing at the edge of the ocean

i need the slightly eroded quicksand moat to protect us all to

sitting on the banks of a new book i abolish your notion of beauty

the sound must never impose itself over the images, or override or

conceptual artists do not march they do not have feet and legs not

i do not claim Black Dada but i know that certain uses of the word

would i be a writer without those who opened up space

The *Black Dada Reader* is a collage by Adam Pendleton in the

internal findings undulate in super slow motion beneath the

in 1960 the poem became a function

the desk is positioned at the wrong height; these goals are a great

back in the dirt: bring a flower when you visit in case the rest is indifferent to the noise of the world

space and upwards a little

criminal the acclimation

which she cannot get up

in post-3.11 Japan

protect us all

shout down

in that way

love is a trap

form of a book

bedroom window

carrier of stillness

unintelligible

she was a proxy for finite differences; she happened at once; she

that bright light where your aesthetics bullies my politics

i am willing to describe you over and over again until you return

not unlike an apology for the atrocities of the American War

a passing moment reveals itself to have been nothing nothing

if empire maps onto bodies, then which limb is your nation

emancipatory and reactionary figures are allowed to coexist

drowning people die quietly while others make some noise

women marched in 2017, in pink hats and not in pink hats

in 1969 Sirhan Sirhan shot Bobby Kennedy no that was 68

Ursonata in the kitchen, Ursonata in the shower

hard to come by a room of my own but i do need some money

destruction is only an opportunity to build and rebuild

refusal to participate in your version of understanding

i don't need to own your words or for that matter mine

if you do not want to be implicated then get out now yes you can radioed

nothing nothing

what i fail to embody can be disbursed and refurbished

that dark alley where my politics beats up your aesthetics

since when is discernment the right thing to desire

i propose an evasion of inordinately large demands

the grand narrative collapses under its own weight

i take a kick in the mouth for you, over and again

the scalpel is sharp, use discretion when cutting

my facility when it arm wrestles with your facility

i let you mortar muzzle celebrate and hate me

speaking into a space where one is illegible

if time drops here my function is to bewilder it

any alerts on the table must answer to the desk

i have solved for x, recall this too is joy

it appears i have made a fine mess of things

on timescales comparable to human lifetimes

i can't metric you no matter how much i try

reflux is the new register upon which we vote

the formal struggle of a vertical field of grass

your transfiguration too controlling for me

the tree of the shade of the leaf of the fall

how will i locate expansiveness in touch

the on-point rhythms of partial identities

no two bodies occupy pink the same way

that's just the way you love, by thinking

back in the dirt: all the loves i have loved

back in the dirt: naïvely rooting around

i don't need your fleabag scuttlebutt

what is globally fluid just think just think

the extent that we need another dollar

i let you fall here like an intimate leaf

and i will share this room with you

i don't need to be at odds with myself

the steady abiding, the deafgain

how can i make this wave speak

for you my friend a little discount

you you you night you you

do you know what i fail like

a fullness and mouth for two

a breakdown of the criteria

destabilize this publication

Ursonata sung by a beetle

the desk is a spatial deadline

no music without friendship

illegible man, irrisible man

i need you to see it, want it

poppycock aperture power

do you want more protection

now i am at odds with myself

we want to make noise

incontinental embodiment

you you you you you fire

performance never dies

alone over my dead fire

Mariana Roa Oliva is going away

lipstick transmission light

Black Dada is not mine

solitude of my pitch

no and no don't die

i need an explanation

pulmonata, kidney of

kick in my mouth

no normalized anger

burnt confabulation

what about dinner

gravitational light

best-case lightbeam

you were elegyfight

evacuate this text

cede of control

line, hold to it

fish or cigarettes

do you like it

prohibitive light

do you hear it

the defiance

we ate them

time capsule

so do i love

light in haste

no language

are you here

Black Dada

no landfill

bed of fog

is it here

refuge

A'

1

it was a wave, would i snap

2

it was a wave, would i snap, was it you

or was it a passing moment of genre trouble, long bewildered

3

it was a wave, would i snap, was it you

sliding between the heat of no and no dislocation

a gasping moment of trouble caught in the bright light

of delay and transitory and loss, hers and mine both

4

it was a wave, one snapped, who blistered

passing moment reveals itself to have extinguished the
occasional light

that turned stranger into child

sliding between ceremony

and languagelight

world without cold

the specs of a body

and the extent to which it delivers

5

it was a wave, it was infectious

an occasional moment reveals nothing but a passing light

extent to which i breathe your facts

it's haptic; it's your membrane; it's material clatter

sliding between your stargazing hoax and flesh

and then somebody steals your wild you

and names it

after a sharp thought

a quiet neck is often indifferent to the mismeasured noise of
the world

substrata lower than the territory concedes

sharp pointed arrows indicate the lack of an end

simulated spacial deadline

a hip, stigmata, shake

she was a threnody hit; she happened; she pitched

i did love it

geometry of pleasure

6

was it hardly a wave

collimation dreams of narrowing waves

the consolidation of my particulate odds

sliding between dreamlight and the way it rolls off

she was elegylight and circumstance; she pitched her light
away

and bid you love

previous utterance catches in the memory like death

closer to the range, the table, the unrepentant tongue

English utters a line for the dead

and then somebody is mouthing my kick

it's haptic; it's your normalized membrane

cantilevered muscles in the backyard of my body

extent that we need another resolution

atop a sharp pink hat, Emma Post just went away

some things don't die so easy

i want the drifting organisms of the ongoing intermission

i want Amber DiPietra and Denise Leto's *Waveform* to
protect us from heavy waves

i want a decidedly animal resolution, J K Chukwu and
Stacey Tran are here but they too will leave, others crowd in
at the last minute

a higher concentration of my predicate silence is cause for a
crash, that would be me

positioned at odds with myself

she was a function of x, her geometry projective; light while
there is light which is now gone

the growing concept of her back

the formal struggle of a line on fire

who and where, why all of a sudden? Adam Golaski went
away again

i have a very animal claim, a brick and mortar politics

yes we are erotic warm anemone

when the sun is saluted, all interventions are off

i think that some people just have no history of art

sediments and molecules burn up in the present moment

hip replacing humans

internal findings crawl back in the dirt and undulate out
while you

cede your control

7

it was a wave all along

in the weight of the moment i am told not to pursue

sliding between detachment, casual surrender, distant
musculatures

of my odd and invisible self

she was a clarity function, a catastrophe; she claimed and
pitched high

the formal struggle of a vertical field of grass

and then somebody grasps it and slips it to you

i need the drifting organisms of the quag to persist

i need the mired waveforms to protect their own selves

i need a Black Dada resolution

cantilevered narratives

there is a stillness when i listen, stop moving and hear the
foul

some people are hit men neverending

Black Dada, Ursonata

this is a snap and tether, i assure it won't drown you

to drown is to impose impolite noises upon your mouth,
head raring back

my nice dick, the sky blue

i want you to see it, to want it, the warm sky

we are warm yes; i quiet the edges of your body into a spin

i need a very animal claim

it's haptic; it's your membrane; it's your unfulfilled threats

it's you dancing in a body that is threatening to whom

an intervention had you requested it

how are we expected to define fulfillment

what makes you wave at my drifting organism

what does it take for you to go all in

to translate that shark, that manatee into your body and its
deepest

do you want the detached musculature to resist the bright
lights

do you need an explanation

what did you say when the grass turned vertical

hip replacing hip

developing scab

internal findings take your highest temperature and toss it
out the window

cede of control

incomplete narrator turns up the volume against the position
the inhabitants the disappearance

the goal of stillness is to link the spectral and the membrane
to a higher form of visibility

uninvited noise is to be held back alongside the other
creatures

we don't want to make your kind of noise

she was a zeta function; she happened again; she is not yet convinced

i need to center an unsolved problem

i need a constant morning, a kick in my mouth or coffee

a jar of silence for two

body with transparent terms

triangle

Black Dada is a way to talk about the future while talking about the past; it is our present moment

a slip of concentration in the predicate vicinity; Theadora Walsh has gone away

magical girls in their colors

did your hue rearrange

the steady abiding deafgain

insert arrow

so did i love

the deadline is a space of time

the wrong height takes its position

line, do your thing

closer to change

i want to drown then laugh

blade then field

self and self

path towards comfort

how will i locate expansiveness in touch

refuse

snap

we are them

8

it was a wave just the waves, the outer sidewalk on my sleeve

she was a bluegreen function; she happened to fall; she pitched the wrong deep

it costs money to get to the bottom of things

the formal struggle of a vertical field of grass, endless and unmarked and i have no trouble with that

now i am at odds with myself my feet are tied

i ask you who said what

Black Dada was written by Adam Pendleton

The *Black Dada Reader* is a collage by Adam Pendleton in the form of a book

Black Dada is not mine, but I undertake *Experiments in Joy*

Black Dada made this book it crashes into my performance
Tuesday May 14 2019 11:50 am

can you hold it, Netop

do you hear it, péngyou

is it hard enough, yūjin

do you like it, Maya Bjornson came and went but left
something behind

do you want more, kaibigan

is this the right angle, vän

is it here, chingu

are you breathing, vriend

is it you, arkadaş

are you here, ffrind

does it hold to the bounds of the circumstance

is it too heavy in light of the actual transgression

what about dinner, tonight

fish or cigarettes for later

or coffee

fog of ours

i cannot claim Black Dada but i know that certain uses of the word love is a trap

internal findings move me close to the bedroom window, i am on the lookout for approaching oceans

art in institutions, institutions in art

slacken and retreat, the new register upon which we vote

music was invented by children to quickly identify who we should love

one can aspire to be either children or sonatas

back in the dirt: aesthetically real flowers

back in the dirt: finite political differences

back in the dirt: all the dirt i have loved

back in the dirt: bring a flower when you visit, i will fix it for you

you you you night you you

that is what she said

i need you to see it, want it, super slowly and resolutely

i need a lower resolution

i need the impending waves to wash away the moat already

i need to enter the alley where we will settle our debts

i need your lilting nocturne to finish marking up the map of
my body

in the late 1960s everybody had a manifesto to write

in 1967 Solanas published her SCUM and LeWitt his
Paragraphs

in 68 Sirhan Sirhan shot Bobby Kennedy

2019 i sit here alone with the fires i love

these are the waves, i pursue my better self

white waves, black waves

in 1970 Irina Dunn shaved her head

in 1960 the poem grew legs

give women more money not hats

i've got dada like a river like a fountain, love like a dada in my
soul in my soul

the 1960s are hungry ghosts loitering around the hot bosom
of the 2010s

i still like Stein but her ego just smacked me in the face

seemingly large beauty or glitter or the dark whip of power

in the wake of the wake of accumulated war neverending war

mass breathing holes

dislocation indignation

burnt confabulation

yo Americano

conceptual artists do not hold hands they do not have hands
not in that way

conceptual artists do not march they do not have feet and
legs not in that way

conceptual artists do not make faces they do not have
feelings not in that way

history is a cube in the foreground i am not a conceptual
artist

you you you you you fire

crashing one wave after another

line, break it

closer to feeling the heat

i want the detached musculature to resist being forced to reattach

kick in the mouth my mouth

i want you to use discretion when cutting my person my drowning my mirror my laughter

i let you insert pointed arrows in spite of no sparkle

so do i love i did love

i will resolve the desk; you can work on the millennium problems

you have made a fine mess, i will stretch it for you

the central rhythms of partial lifetimes

the sound must never impose itself

anything on the table must answer to the metric

emancipatory and reactionary figures vying to coexist

substandard caprice, horrid little boys, and schooners of any kind are actively discouraged and sooner transfigured the tree of the shade of the leaf of the fall

expansiveness in hybrid bodies are touching me all over

an intervention or a way of showing love

when i was willing to wait thirty minutes, two hours, ten years for you

sharp blade of a dirty field

fall into fall

cantilever this

your facts fill it up

scrap

deluge

a quiet neck is often discomfiting, all that is indifferent to the noise of the world

the assumption of her failure

how will I locate expansiveness in touch

the extent that we feed another creature

do you think that if i brought you more and more

if time falls illegible my function is to recoup it

i need a newer explanation

better able to introduce a path towards friendship

Black Dada is our present moment

not canceling means keeping some waves afloat in the spine
of my final body

that is to say i need you to see it, want it

the solitude of my commitments

a mortar and muzzle politics

the steady abiding, the deafgain

time capsule

we want to make a certain noise

hip replacement hip

internal motions beneath the bedroom window

cede of control

imperialist narrator turns the volume up against the position
the principle the susurration

i need a porous morning, a kick in my mouth for the steep
tune of decay

a fullness and mouth for two dead fires

i propose we escape their reality

no i do not speak Dada

the ringing sound you hear

is a higher transmission

since when is transmission the best thing to desire

no and no

what is it that creatures you

sitting on the banks i relinquish my need to attract

a queynte deep in the blue sky

what i fail to embody should be thrown in the can

i suspect you know what i fail like and how this ends

variegate, eat, repeat, i was wrong, you can say it, so get up

i am no longer at odds with myself

solitude of my word, be good

pitch it to you

NOTES & ACKNOWLEDGEMENTS

Some forms of loss are legible, others are complicated by their own illegibility. *Pink Waves* wrote itself from and towards the unstable intersections of love, grief, loss, and joy. An illegible loss of a child. Cancellation of waves and other matter. Detritus thereby left in limbo.

The first text that called *Pink Waves* into being was the book *Waveform* by Amber DiPietra and Denise Leto. *Pink Waves* accrues lines written in conversation with *Waveform*, together with what I call microtranslations of syntax in "Black Dada" by Adam Pendleton. "Microtranslation" is a term I invented to refer to the act of translating some, but not all, aspects of a text. Translation as an ancient, emergent genre.

Lately when I am asking what form a poem wants to inhabit, it is often syntax that leads the way. In Adam Pendleton's *Becoming Imperceptible*, I heard a quiet syntax of repeating images—a syntax later echoed in language in his poem, "Black Dada," which also appeared in *The Supposium* (edited by Joan Retallack)—all of which helped *Pink Waves* find its form. Through "Black Dada" I heard the underlying structure of Ron Silliman's *Ketjak*, like the bass line from a familiar song. I heard the timbre and edge of Amiri Baraka's voice— "money, God, power/a moral code, so cruel." Sometimes I quoted directly from my source text: "Black Dada is a way to talk about the future while talking about the past; it is our present moment." It is a cacophonous present moment, but I find quietness here too. In *Waveform* I heard the sounds of bodies in suspension, bodies in writing. They write: "I am just using words to touch places in my body that have gone numb, quiet, crunched."

Pink Waves is a structured improvisation: the form, the sentence, the microtranslation, the language from the sources, are the structure with which I improvised in writing, on stage, with others. It is my attempt to be true to the thickness as I move through time and space, in cross-sections of wave upon wave. Some forms of otherness are more specific to my own history, some arrive through the discourse of others. All these spreading differences.

SOURCES: *Waveform* by Amber DiPietra and Denise Leto (Kenning Editions, 2011); "Black Dada" by Adam Pendleton, from *Becoming Imperceptible* (Siglio, 2016) and also *The Supposium*, edited by Joan Retallack (Litmus Press, 2018); *Ketjak* and *Sunset Debris* by Ron Silliman, as collected in *The Age of Huts* (UC Press, 2007). Warm thanks to the authors of these texts for their kind support of this project and its engagements.

MANY THANKS: to the editors of the print and online publications in which excerpts of the book have appeared—*Poetry, The White Review, Academy of American Poets/Poem-a-Day*.

MAY 2019 WRITING PERFORMANCE: May 14th to May 16th, 2019, 9 am to 5 pm, McCormack Family Theater at Brown University. Gale Nelson, Jenny Witt, and Jesse Tessier—thank you for enabling the performance, and thanks also to those who participated or helped me break it down.

THANKS: to Rae Armantrout, Gabrielle Civil, Chris Clemans, Madhu H. Kaza, Christine Sun Kim, Violet Ace Harlo, Andria Hickey, Steven Rood, Jennifer Scappettone. To MacDowell, where I wrote the "Notes." To my students and colleagues at Brown University.

SPECIAL THANKS: Colin Channer, John Granger, Fred Moten, Joan Retallack.

OMNIDAWN: Warmest and infinite thank yous to Rusty Morrison and Ken Keegan. To Laura Joakimson. To Kayla Ellenbecker, Ashley Pattison-Scott, Rob Hendricks, and the entire team at Omnidawn.

LOVE: Always, to Eugene, Marina, Jona. To my parents, brother, extended, chosen.

COVER ART

Borrowed Landscape VIII (humid continental climate, summer)
Naomi Kawanishi Reis
Mixed media on washi and mylar
26 x 20 inches   2020

Sawako Nakayasu is an artist working with language, performance, and translation – separately and in various combinations. Her books, pamphlets, and translations include *Some Girls Walk Into The Country They Are From, Say Translation Is Art, The Ants*, and the translation of *The Collected Poems of Chika Sagawa*, as well as *Mouth: Eats Color – Sagawa Chika Translations, Anti-translations, & Originals*. She teaches at Brown University.

photo: Mitsuo Okamoto

Pink Waves

by Sawako Nakayasu

Cover art by Naomi Kawanishi Reis

Interior typeface: Adobe Jenson Pro
Cover and Interior design by Sawako Nakayasu and Laura Joakimson

Printed in the United States
by Books International, Dulles, Virginia
on Acid Free Archival Quality Recycled Paper

Publication of this book was made possible in part by gifts from
Katherine & John Gravendyk in honor of Hillary Gravendyk,
Francesca Bell, Mary Mackey, and The New Place Fund

Omnidawn Publishing
Oakland, California
Staff and Volunteers, Spring 2022

Rusty Morrison & Ken Keegan, senior editors & co-publishers
Laura Joakimson, production editor and poetry & fiction editor
Rob Hendricks, editor for *Omniverse*, poetry & fiction, & post-pub marketing,
Sharon Zetter, poetry editor & book designer
Jeff Kingman, copy editor
Liza Flum, poetry editor
Anthony Cody, poetry editor
Jason Bayani, poetry editor
Gail Aronson, fiction editor
Jennifer Metsker, marketing assistant
Jordyn MacKenzie, marketing assistant
Sophia Carr, marketing assistant